living with **white**

living with white

decorating with shades of white, texture, and accents of color

gail abbott
photography by **mark scott**

CICO BOOKS
LONDON NEW YORK

For my mother

Published in 2009 by CICO Books
An imprint of Ryland Peters & Small Ltd
20–21 Jockey's Fields   519 Broadway, 5th Floor
London WC1R 4BW   New York, NY 10012

www.cicobooks.com

10 9 8 7 6 5 4 3 2 1

Text © Gail Abbott 2009
Design and photography © CICO Books 2009

A CIP catalog record for this book is available from the Library
of Congress and the British Library.

ISBN-13: 978 1 906525 24 8

Printed in China

Editor: Gillian Haslam
Designer: Christine Wood
Photographer: Mark Scott

contents

introduction

White is one of the most widely-used shades in the modern palette, and with good reason. Pure, fresh, and peaceful, a white room can be used as a stylish backdrop to many different types of interior. In its purest form, white is used to make dark rooms look spacious and airy, reflecting what little light is allowed in. White is also used in modernist homes that rely on clean lines and contemporary styling. Dark wooden floors, white-painted furniture, the natural textures of a thatched roof, or the aged surface of reclaimed teak—all these can be teamed with white and all bring a unique style to an unassuming space. Combining white with color can be dazzling in a sunny climate, and painting one wall of an all-white room with brilliant color can have the effect of bringing the outside in, especially if a second shade is introduced as an accent.

Texture is used in a poolside wall built of brick and washed with stucco, found in the use of natural white linen or a twisted natural vine used for a handrail on a staircase. These are whites filtered through the hand of nature and are often used in conjunction with the palest of polished concrete, so beloved of contemporary designers.

This book looks at many different styles of houses that rely on white for their impact. A cubist beach house on the Gulf coast of Florida is a modernist dream of glass and concrete, while the white rooms of a converted winery on the island of Santorini, with tiny windows to keep out the heat, are filled with light. From a unique farmhouse in South Africa that combines different textures with white to a high-rise condo with cutting edge design that sits above the bright lights of Miami, this book explores the work of architects and designers who have used modern and traditional materials like concrete, adobe, steel, and plaster to build homes that integrate with the surrounding landscape. In hot and humid climates, living outdoors is essential, and white stucco and bleached hardwoods are used to brilliant effect for swimming pools, sun decks, cool terraces, and containing walls. Take inspiration from the diversity of styles and materials discovered within these pages and use white for your own stylish and individual home.

chapter one

island whites

keeping cool

Island dwellers throughout the centuries have adapted to the particular conditions in which they find themselves, and on the Cycladic Greek islands the inhabitants have had two major elements to contend with—the searing heat of noon in midsummer and the strong, hot August winds, called the "meltemi," that blow in from the Aegean Sea. Householders need plenty of protection from both these elements and they have devised traditional ways of keeping cool and sheltering from the wind. One of these is to build village houses close together, each dwelling surrounded by a high, startlingly white wall.

left: Brilliant magenta against the traditional white walls is provided by riotous bougainvillea blossoms that bloom around every corner. Doors are painted blue, a traditional color intended to keep away evil spirits and which makes such a vivid contrast to the white walls.

right: A typically Greek scene on the Cycladic island of Santorini, the brilliant white walls contrast with the blue of the sky and provide a shady walkway through the village.

As the sun gets lower and temperatures drop, sitting on a high terrace overlooking the sea is a pleasure to be enjoyed every evening in the town of Fira on Santorini. Sunset-watching is a popular activity, and hundreds of vacationers gather along west-facing terraces at sundown to admire the panorama as the fiery red ball sinks into the sea. The town is built completely of white houses and blue domed-churches—the epitome of Greek island living, and white really comes into its own as the light fades. The pristine stucco of the small square houses that cluster across the hillside assumes a vibrancy as dusk falls, capturing every last gleam of light in that magical transition between day and night.

left: Exposed on the corner of a terrace that in the middle of the day would be too hot for most to enjoy, by early evening the heat has gone. Pale flagstones are set into a flooring of gray pebbles that lighten the corner as the light dims.

right: A white canvas bench seat is tucked under an arbor made from white-painted garden trellis, while Mediterranean plants add color and texture. The graphic black-and-white pillows add a contemporary note to the setting, with its marble table top and slatted park seats.

alfresco living

One of the joys of living or vacationing on a sunny island is the opportunity to eat outside practically all year round. In the Greek islands it's possible to sit out at any time of day during winter months, but the heat of summer requires the judicious use of white canvas awnings to provide essential shade when the sun reaches its zenith. In a tiny courtyard hidden behind a pale plastered wall, traditional white deckchairs and an oversized white parasol deflect the heat of the sun, providing a welcome place to sit and enjoy a relaxed meal under cover, while waiting for the midday heat to abate.

left: Zonal pelargoniums, more often known as geraniums, thrive in the heat of a Greek summer. Planted in containers of every shape and size, they are seen around every corner on doorsteps and in terraced gardens. Planted in an enormous terracotta pot, a bright pink variety makes a colorful display against the pale walls.

right: A combination of natural stone and the local plasterwork, or "patito," has been used to construct this high wall round the courtyard. The yard underfoot is laid with a mixture of light pebbles in varying tones of gray and white.

left: With the influx of European buyers, many traditional houses on Greek and Mediterranean islands have been converted into second homes and sometimes given a surprising new look. Rounding a corner in a remote island village, one is dazzled by the contrast between the pink and yellow walls and the more conventional blue of the door.

right: On a hilly island, many of the lanes are on a steep gradient, and toiling up numerous steps is one of the facts of island life. In these steep and narrows lanes, many of which are totally inaccessible by car, the locals still use donkeys for deliveries of building materials. The concrete steps are outlined in white so no-one loses their footing.

moorish influence

As the Greek island of Santorini became more and more popular as a tourist resort, many of the traditional homes in the rural villages, as well as in the main towns, have been converted into luxury vacation villas. At Villa Io, in Megalachori, the original courtyard of a simple artisan's dwelling has been almost filled with a splendid new swimming pool hidden behind its high, terracotta-colored walls.

The influence of the thousands of tourists from Europe and the rest of the world who have flooded the island since the opening of an international airport in the 1970s, has brought many contemporary design

below: The muslin drapes of the daybed billow gently in the breeze and make a dreamy canopy over the canvas-covered pillows. Knotted in the corners, the sweep of the drapes is held back, providing shade without restricting the view of the pool.

below: As the sun moves round and the pool is partly in shadow, the white daybed seems particularly inviting in the shady corner. The walls are high enough to make sure that one end of the courtyard is out of the sun even at noon, so both sun-lovers and shade-seekers are catered for.

styles to these once remote islands. These pink plastered walls reflect a love of traditional Moroccan style that is now cropping up all around the world, from South Africa to California and Australia—a decorating style that has found fertile soil in the hot, sunny islands of the Mediterranean and the Aegean. The deep, rich color makes for a sophisticated ambience that allows the romantic white muslin drapes of the daybed to promise a cool and welcoming refuge from the sun after a refreshing dip in the pool, and is a feature that brings an exotic "Arabian Nights" vibe to the space.

traditionally white

Finding a shady place to relax in the middle of the day often means coming inside for a quiet rest, and traditional island houses are designed to stay cool without the benefits of modern air conditioning and ceiling fans. Thick white walls, pale plaster floors, and tiny windows all mean that the interiors of island homes throughout the centuries have been kept at a level temperature all year round. Nothing is left to chance, and it's a design that has been used since the earliest civilizations. Everything is intended to keep the elements at bay and no detail is there for purely aesthetic reasons. At Villa Io, the conventional island vernacular style is seen in the tiny windows each side of the heavy timber doors, designed to keep out the heat and the currents from the strong winds. The interior rooms are all pure white, a device that helps make the tiny spaces look much larger, and reflects whatever light enters through the door and windows.

left: The traditional "patito" plasterwork is seen in the construction of the outside steps that lead to a storage area and the warm pink contrasts comfortably with the pure white of the interior.

right: Converted into a relaxing place to spend vacations, this traditional island home has retained all the elements that keep it so cool. White linen slip covers, white-plastered walls, and simple furniture add to the feeling of peace and tranquility.

elemental forces

The island of Santorini is the site of one of the largest volcanic eruptions ever known, one which occurred 3,600 years ago and is thought to have destroyed the ancient Minoan civilization on the island of Crete, 100 miles to the south. Consequently, most of the island is made up of volcanic lava. The islanders have always made the most of this soft material by excavating "cave" homes into the hillsides, merely building a wall across the tunneled-out space and fitting a door and a couple of windows to the front. These simple, vaulted dwellings are still in use, and their curved interior lines are plastered with a resilient white finish. It's an ideal way to build in this climate, giving protection from heat and wind, and imparting a purity to the churchlike spaces. Timber is a rare luxury on this bare volcanic island, so later building methods emulated this same style, with houses built from stone and using local volcanic ash mixed with water as cement. Vaulted ceilings are constructed with concrete over wire mesh, a technique that allows movement in case of earth tremors.

left: Many of the floors have sustained minor cracks that snake their way across the surface of the plaster, testament to the low-level earthquakes of the region. With the interior surfaces smooth and uncluttered, furniture is often minimal and similarly plain. Here, the cool, white canvas sofa covers are easily removed for washing, and the only splash of color is provided by the pair of citrus green pillows.

above: A pendant light has been made from one of the vines that produce the famous Santorini wines. Because of the strong winds on the island in summer, the vines are trained on the ground into low basket-shaped crowns and the grapes grow inside these as protection. This ancient vine circle has been decorated with a metallic leaf garland and fitted with low-voltage spotlights before being suspended from chains, where it adds a theatrical touch to the white ceiling.

Many of the traditional houses of the Aegean islands have been converted into vacation villas and apartments and fitted out in a contemporary style. So much so that the older style of island furniture is becoming much less popular. The local owner of this house wanted to keep one foot in the past and has found ways of using antique Greek furniture, and even a certain amount of recycling, to bring in elements that are familiar from his island childhood. Throughout the house old pieces of wood and furniture have been pressed into service in unusual and innovative ways—an antique carved door has become a tabletop, an old window lock has been made into a towel rail, and in the dining area a vintage set of table and chairs gives an authentic edge to the airy white-plastered room. All the essentials for keeping cool are in place in the kitchen—the small, shuttered windows, the heavy wooden door, and the high window above it for ventilation.

left: In the kitchen, the high white ceiling is especially necessary to let the heat rise away from the cooking area. The kitchen may have been refurbished with modern cooking appliances, but the age-old techniques for keeping cool still apply.

far right: Contrasting with the white-domed room and the pale distressed mirror frame, the antique table and chairs bring with them solidity and a link with the past.

right: Above the worktop, the white walls have been half-plastered with the same terracotta plaster as the cupboards below. An old chair back is pressed into service as an unusual utensil rack.

a tranquil sanctuary

The grapes that grow on the rich, volcanic soil of Santorini produce distinctive wines that have been made on the island for centuries. Many of the older wineries, or "kanavas," have now been converted into chic retreats for the sophisticated tourists who flock to the island, and Blue Angel Villa, in the main town of Fira, is one of these.

The building's origin as a kanava is seen in the soaring vaulted ceiling, and the high white space that was carved out of the rock of the island makes it an especially cool and peaceful retreat. When the Athens-based owners took it over, the eighteenth-century building had fallen into disrepair, and had long since ceased operating as a business. Making the most of the height, a white-painted wooden mezzanine level makes a comfortable bedroom space and the high arched window was instaled in the curve of the roof to allow in extra light.

left: With all-white walls, furniture, and woodwork, and with cool, handmade Italian floor tiles, the villa makes a tranquil sanctuary from the busy streets outside. Another window in the dining area has been added beside the door, allowing in a little more light that glows as it floods the interior space. In its former life there were no windows, just a pair of heavy wooden doors through which cartloads of grapes would have been brought inside.

left: In the dining area, the minimal furnishings are all designed to be easy to keep clean. A set of white canvas covers can be washed on a hot cycle and bleached in the sun to keep them pristine.

right: The heavy white painted table was made by a carpenter in Athens to the owner's design and shipped over to the island by ferry.

light and white

The interior of Blue Angel Villa was originally dark and gloomy with no natural light at all, carved as it was out of the volcanic hillside in the traditional way of Santorini "cave" houses. It needed a calculated redesign to turn it from an industrial building into a serene and light-filled contemporary dwelling.

There is no way for light to enter except through the new windows and doors added at the front when the restoration started. The strong outside light is intensified when reflected off the sea in the caldera below and the neighboring whitewashed houses. Plenty of white surfaces inside ensure that what light does enter is reflected from walls, ceiling, furniture, and woodwork. An all-white interior is a classic solution for making spaces seem lighter and bigger, and whatever light is allowed inside is doubled, taking on a luminous quality. Use contrasting textures and the differences become all the more apparent as light falls across them, making the very whites themselves look different. See how the contrasting textures of the glossy painted tabletop, the rough, matt wood of the beams, and the canvas of the slipcovers absorb or deflect the light. It's a timeless way of making an ancient space look light and contemporary, but one that breathes with the fabric of the building, revealing rather than concealing its history.

sensitive restoration

The upgrade of a traditional building can take many different routes—the owners may decide to keep all the original details, choosing an authentic style of decoration and reproducing colors and furnishings that they assume to have been the interior decorating style; they may sweep everything away and start completely from scratch, inserting a totally fresh interior within the structure, or they might leave the bare bones of the building, incorporating original features and details into the final design with sensitivity and skill.

Into the authentic and open space of this old kanava, a contemporary style fits with ease and grace. The building was sensitively converted from its original format, but the basic structure was left unchanged. Before the conversion, the main room was an empty space with a high, vaulted ceiling, with two completely dark spaces tucked into the area behind,

and a warren of smaller rooms at the side. These rooms have all been left basically intact and the original floor plan unaffected, but a modern ensuite shower room has been instaled into one of the once dark and uninhabitable store rooms, and the addition of a mezzanine level at the front makes an extra bedroom reached by a new wooden staircase. The resulting room is tucked into the roof space, from which a guest has a stunning view over the caldera, the sea-filled volcanic basin.

left: A pastel pleated silk bed cover and pair of white muslin drapes give this bedroom in the roof a touch of romance that turns the open mezzanine floor into a luxurious sleeping platform.

top right: The rounded edges of the shower needed a flexible finish, and using hundreds of small tesserae, or mosaic tiles, made it possible to tile the organic shapes of the design.

right: With its rounded shapes and smooth, plastered finish, the design of the walk-in shower takes its inspiration from the local architecture and needs clever lighting to illuminate it. A mere touch of white in the grouting around the tiles is enough to spark up the various blues of the room.

Adapting an essentially industrial space into a restrained yet comfortable villa demanded a combination of minimalism and luxury. This white, high-ceilinged room is spare and minimal, but splashes of rich sea greens and blues add color and vitality and echo the world outside the front door. Santorini is renowned worldwide for its sparkling white buildings and blue-domed churches, and the turquoise sea that surrounds the island flashes and glitters in the sunlight. The interior decor of the villa is informed by all these elements, combining simplicity and relaxation with touches of glamour. Blending the old with the new takes a restrained hand, so

below left: The new, white wooden staircase rises from the floor of the main room to the sleeping platform on the mezzanine level above. The structure is unpretentious and minimal and links the two levels without fuss.

below: Echoing the cool blues of the tiled floor that runs throughout the villa, the silk pillows and seat cover on the built-in divans add an iridescence that recalls the deep ocean blues of the Aegean Sea.

the basic elements are kept as simple as possible. Bare, plastered walls and a minimalist white staircase (see next page) allow the spirit of the original building to shine through and keep the interior cool. There are no ultra-modern details, but a respect for the functional island architecture leaves the space clear and uncluttered with little or no extraneous decorative elements. Furniture is low and discreet—fitted into the main room, low bench seats serve as couches along the walls, and are an understated way to provide seating that can also double up as extra beds if necessary in the large living area.

below: The back wall of the open living space clearly shows the shape of the high, vaulted ceiling that was formed when the kanava was carved out of the volcanic rock. The new owners pierced the wall with three new windows to let light into the bedroom behind, and the white plaster serves ideally to embrace the curve of the dome.

white arches

Tucked away behind high walls in a typical Greek island village, and hidden from passers-by, another wine maker's building, built in 1856, has been sensitively restored as a modern, open-plan home. The kanava originally belonged to the Gavalas family who are still making wine in the village today.

The structure is low and constructed from local stone rather than carved into the hillside, although the building has all the hallmarks of one of the older buildings and is as cool on a fiercely hot August day as any of the traditional cave homes. The white-plastered ceiling is vaulted, and the stone arches made from the soft island pumice, or "porri," that span the space are left exposed. The few windows are tiny and situated high up in the external wall, and the little light that is allowed in is filtered by the internal wooden shutters that also keep out the dust and sand carried on hot summer winds.

The present owner bought the house as two separate apartments, which she converted into an open-plan area with light-reflecting white walls and floors, and simple, interconnected living, eating, and bathing spaces. The arched wall was opened up, restoring the space to its initial floor plan, and it is the present owner who designed the innovative bathroom fittings with their quirky combination of ancient form and modern utility.

right: Contemporary rattan furniture imported from Indonesia, a set of striking blue-and-white striped pillows made locally, and crisp white bed linen keep the interior of the house fresh and modern and echo the brilliant blue and white of the surrounding buildings.

all in the detail

Conventional methods of building traditional homes were necessarily simple for most islanders, and the best vernacular architecture is a time-tested response to the environment. With no natural forests, using timber was out of the question, so it was the local volcanic deposits that provided the porous stone used for building the three-feet-thick walls that keep the houses remarkably cool in summer and warm in winter. In older-style interiors, especially those of workplaces such as a kanava, the stone walls would have been left unplastered, the interior being mostly dark. But the restoration of an old structure for use as a contemporary

below left: A simple mirror sits on a shelf constructed from a piece of driftwood, and the rounded contours of the bath are finished in the traditional white waterproof plaster. The huge storage jar used as a basin was made locally and is a reproduction of one found nearby where the ancient city of Akrotiri is being excavated.

below: Water for the shower gushes from a brick carved from porri, or porous pumice stone, into the Roman-style shallow bath. Without a swimming pool in the courtyard, the shower is a convenient way to keep cool in the middle of a hot day.

home means that white patito plaster covers the walls and floors, reflecting maximum light and giving the open spaces a feeling of airiness, even though the actual amount of natural light is minimal.

The owner of this house has looked to the history of the Greek civilization for inspiration for the understated decorations that bring such a sense of place. The ancient-looking "pithoi," or ceramic storage jars, are a combination of reproduction and antique, with one or two pieces found in the building when it was originally converted. The pieces bring subtle and understated touches to the interior that evoke a real sense of history.

below: Against the plain white walls, no attempt has been made to decorate in a conventional way. There are no pictures or curtains, and no elaborate light fittings dilute the purity of form, so the beautiful spaces and local artefacts are left to speak for themselves.

ice blue and white

In a low-key conversion of an island home, a spacious bathroom has been instaled in place of the original kitchen. The room is unique, without a straight line to be seen, and the owner has included evidence of the house's history that allows the past to shine through, bringing with it a distinctive sense of atmosphere.

The deep alcove that contains the spa bath and shower has been rendered with cool, pale blue plaster, an age-old treatment for walls both inside and out that is shared with the traditional building techniques of Morocco. The polished plaster catches the light and gives a waterproof finish that shines from within and brings the smooth surface alive. It is a time-honored finish that is being used for bathrooms the world over by interior designers in place of more conventional tiling, and one that looks incredibly fresh and contemporary in this simple peasant dwelling. In the corner of the bath, a rough piece of stone pierces the smooth finish of the plaster and is confirmation that the room was carved out of the soft stone of the island when the house was first constructed. Antique artefacts, like the carved wooden door used as a low table, and the slender metal window catch now doing service as a towel rail, all add immeasurably to the character and mood.

left: The dark wooden antiques contrast with the pale blue-plastered bath and walls and give a focus to the otherwise cool, watery interior. White towels are folded on the dark table, softening the lines and adding a feeling of luxury and comfort.

chapter two

contemporary whites

below: A twentieth-century design classic, the white Verner Panton chair is a single, fluid shape made from molded polypropylene, which is perfect for use outside in the shallows of the pool.

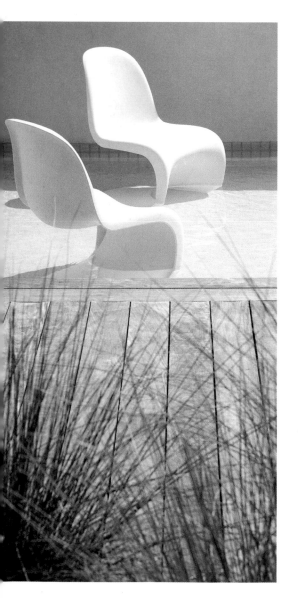

cool pools

The hot and humid Florida summer means that many contemporary homes have a swimming pool where residents can cool off after a day in the office. Private pools are sometimes simply a modestly narrow strip, enabling a few enervating laps up and down, and sometimes they are more lavish, large enough to splash and play under the gush of a refreshing fountain.

Under the glare of the southern summer sun, the use of white reflects the light and transforms a pool area or relaxation deck into a tranquil oasis. Filled with water, a white pool turns to pale azure as it reflects the arc of the sky above, transforming it with an allure that invites one to laze in the cooling water, or to simply sit and observe the light sparkling across the ripples. Interior designer Ken Ganeaux collaborated with the owners when it came to designing this luxury pool with its three mini-waterfalls and gently rising steps. The project was for a modern, but not modernist, house in Rosemary Beach, on the Emerald Coast in Florida. Rosemary Beach is a fast-growing beach community, and houses are rising quickly outside the sheltering wall of the garden that affords a degree of privacy to bathers. The wall, pool, and steps have all been given the same white stucco finish that lends smoothness to the surface and allows a gentle gradation of blue as the water gets deeper. The most unusual feature is the shallow sitting area, where you can relax for a few moments with feet cooling in the water.

right: The blue and white of the pool keeps its freshness and purity with the minimum of maintenance in the hot Florida sunshine. The thick stucco wall has an elegantly shaped curve that fits effortlessly round the shape of the pool, and narrow pierced slits that break up the bare expanse of stucco.

outdoor living

This contemporary house in Rosemary Beach, designed by architect Carey McWhorter, has only recently been completed and is a departure from the modernist houses he has built elsewhere in the area. Local planners encourage a mix of styles to give the development character and a sense of a community that is growing organically. The high-pitched roof extends over the courtyard, allowing it to double up as a sitting area all year round, and the pale stucco wall that wraps the house and garden is tall and sheltering. The pierced slits let in strong shafts of sunlight that move dramatically across the wall and show chinks of the neighboring houses. It's a theatrical light show that depends on the whiteness of the wall for its full effect.

below left: The garden has been planted with typically tropical species by designer Dana Hicks. Plants like agave, rosemary, santolina, and wax myrtle provide a rich blend of shapes that throw into relief the strong white verticals of the house's structure.

below: The reclaimed teak garden table is left outside all year, so numerous summers have scoured the wood and bleached it to a pale gray-white. Piled with classically-styled white china, the dining table recedes into the background, allowing the soft colors of the garden to take center stage.

right: In carefully chosen shades of citrus and gray, pillows add understated color to the white bench seat and wall behind. Sunbrella, an all-weather fabric designed for boat awnings, was used for the pillow covers to withstand the fading effects of sun and rain.

classic contemporary

A white-painted room has become one of the most popular decorating classics—it is guaranteed not to go out of fashion, and never looks dated. But it's important to think about the judicious use of texture and color if an all-white room is not to be merely a blank, featureless space. Having white as your starting point means that color can be added as interesting accents that will underline and stand out against the monochrome background. As color trends rise and fall, it's easy to substitute a pair of pillows or a set of new bed linen without completely redecorating, and textures can be introduced in the form of drapes or shades, rugs, and upholstery fabrics, while accessories like lamps and wall art will bring the

whole look together. White has become a classic backdrop to an international style that relies on clean lines, a dash of subtle color, and dark accessories.

Richly colored walnut floors run throughout the interior of this Rosemary Beach house. Designer Ken Ganeaux has worked with a two-tone scheme of white and dark brown, enlivened by a pair of chartreuse pillows that provide the only color accent. When the core pairings are so simple, texture plays its part. The suede-effect bed head and chair pillows, woven furniture, and raised-pile rug build up layers of surface textures that weave the overall style together.

left: Ultrasuede, used here on the bed head and chair seats, was the first microfiber fabric and was introduced in 1970. It feels just like suede but is totally resistant to stains, won't pull or fray, and can be laundered in the washing machine, making it perfect for all interior projects.

right: Sunlight streams into the bedroom through the floor-to-ceiling glass doors that overlook the pool. Curtains are deliberately understated and the only colors used are brown and white, except for the subtlest glimpse of chartreuse in the prints that echoes the bed pillows.

The primary concept for the design was to build a house that looked as though it had originally been a working building—a warehouse, say, or a barn, although the area around Rosemary Beach was virgin territory until 1995 when the new beach-side town was born. The bare bones of the structure have been deliberately left uncovered to go along with the intended impression of a house with history.

The structure of the roofline has been kept simple, with darkly stained roof trusses and beams left exposed, and an internal cladding of white-painted tongue-and-groove boarding. Insulation has been fitted behind the cladding under the corrugated metal roof, making the house as environmentally friendly as possible. Corrugated steel is a roofing material used extensively in Florida due to the gale force or hurricane winds that are prone to strip traditional tiles off a roof in minutes, and it's a finish that gives more weight to the idea of an industrial provenance to the building.

Internally, walnut is a wood finish that recurs throughout the unadorned, white painted rooms—in the glossy strip flooring, in the doors to every room, and in the bespoke cabinets in the bathrooms designed by Ganeaux and built in situ by a local joiner. Plain white bathroom fittings from Italy add to the no-frills concept. It's a house whose design is uncompromisingly unassuming—simple, modern, and unembellished.

left: Sitting in solitary splendor, and as beautiful and moving as a modern sculpture on the gallery-white landing, Ken Ganeaux has placed a vintage wooden chair that he found on Ebay, a rich hunting ground for unusual and individual pieces of furniture.

top right: Adding to the Zen-like atmosphere of simplicity and restraint, a white ceramic Buddha head gives an air of serenity to the bathroom.

bottom right: The stylish white wall lights are the classic "Ariel" fittings, from Artemide. A single light fitted into the wall of mirror gives the impression of a pair and doubles the light output.

less is more

Surrounded by a lush tropical garden, the steel and glass home of Terence Riley and John Bennett in Miami is a tribute to the modernist ideas of the German-born architect, Ludwig Mies van der Rohe. The original inspiration was a house with a central courtyard that Mies designed but never built, and the main ingredients are the steel and glass structures that he propounded in the 1940s.

The house has an inward-looking aspect; built around a central courtyard with a sliver of a blue lap pool, the bedrooms are reached via a slim bridge that crosses the water, and the abiding impression is one of light and space.

right: The flat roof overhangs the kitchen and living room by eight feet, keeping the interior cool and shady in summer. The walls are built of concrete blocks covered with white stucco and in-filled with sliding glass doors.

below left: The owners carefully calibrated the effect of the light as it moves around the house and courtyard, even going so far as to make a computer simulation to get an exact impression. The result is a moving play of intense light and shadow against the minimal white walls.

below: In the courtyard, a white canvas daybed is heaped with pillows. At night the blank wall opposite is used as an open-air cinema screen.

Set against the brilliant white of both the interior and exterior walls, the glossy orange Bulthaup kitchen units have a clean, sculptural quality that almost belies its use as a workplace. The surface is kept clear and uncluttered, with all food preparation equipment stored well out of sight underneath the stainless steel worktop. The vivid orange of the cabinets contrasts with the blown-up photograph of a vast blue ocean by Richard Misrach, instaled by the artist on the side of the interior cube that houses storage, kitchen cupboards, and a bathroom.

Terence Riley is Director of the Miami Art Museum, and his association with contemporary artists informed his choice of this wall art, one of a few carefully selected pieces of art in the house. The result is a striking reference to Mies van der Rohe who promoted the idea of assimilating art into architecture. True to Mies's stated spiritual goal "To bring Nature, man and architecture together into a higher Unity," the Miami house initiates a dialog between the artificial and the natural.

right: The vivid contrast between the orange of the kitchen units and the ocean blue of the wall art is made more noticeable in the minimal white spaces of the house. The white table is from Saarinen and the gray rubber "Non" chairs are from Komplot.

jungle planting

A high, white rendered wall surrounds the outside of this house, making certain the privacy of the interior, and inside this at both back and front a verdant jungle garden has been planted, rich in tall palms and lush ferns. The walls of glass blur the distinction between inside and out in bedrooms and bathrooms, and provide a playful dialog between nature and architecture. The effect is heightened by the use of small, pale green mosaic tiles in the master shower room, adding to the impression that all daylight entering the room has been filtered by the garden plants.

right: Contained by the walls beyond the garden, the guest bedroom has a serenity caused in part by the way the walls disappear into the jungle foliage. The furniture is white and minimal, with the only touch of color in the red floor-length curtains.

below left: The cool en-suite shower room is lined with green Bisazza mosaic tiles and the polished concrete floor runs into the walk-in shower.

below: A square white wash basin is wall-hung to keep the floor clear and the lines clean, and the lush Cabada palms outside are reflected in the mirror.

left: The tropical gardens were designed by renowned landscape architect Raymond Jungles, who used indigenous palms to create narrow strip gardens outside the glass walls of the house. A native of the Florida Everglades, the light green leaves of the Paurotis palm look impressive when lit up at night and viewed from the interior of the house.

right: There's little to be seen of the house from the road. Set in Miami's Design District, with its tree-lined streets and shady walkways, the house keeps itself to itself behind a white wall shaded by a large specimen of a *Quercas virginiana*, or Southern Live Oak, a native of Florida. Panels of frosted glass maintain the privacy of the inhabitants.

rescued cladding

In the watery swamps of Florida and the Mississippi grows the North American Cypress, the wood of which is popular for interior paneling and flooring. Some cypress trees are attacked by a fungus that enters the trunk and branches, forming lens-shaped pockets that create a beautiful three-dimensional, textured effect in the wood, called Pecky cypress, when planked. Designer Ken Ganeaux used this wood to line the walls and ceilings of his outdoor dining room and personally selected the trees as they were pulled from the swamp.

right: The doors to the house fold right back, forming one large room with no boundary between inside and out. The interior walls are finished with white stucco.

below: Sitting at the Indonesian table in the paneled loggia gives a feeling of being in a cigar box. The distinctively textured cypress wood on walls and ceiling reduces glare from the sun for outdoor diners in the day, and imparts a cosy, intimate ambience at night.

the high life

High up on the twenty-seventh floor of his brand-new condominium, entrepreneur Jeff Morr enjoys spectacular views of Miami, in Florida. It's a vista that stretches from the skyscrapers of downtown Miami in the south to a far distant sighting of Fort Lauderdale in the north. The new development is one of the first to be built in the untouched railroad district of the city. Low, tree-lined streets extend in all directions, but only five minutes away by car is the glittering South Beach, with its hotels, street cafés, roller-blading models, and the renowned Art Deco District.

The deep, long balcony wraps around two sides of the apartment and provides a 180-degree panorama as well as a choice of relaxing in the shade or enjoying the sun on the white canvas loungers. Inside, the rooms are shaded by the projecting roof of the apartment above, a common feature of the modernist buildings that abound in Miami. The view is the main attraction, but the sky-high position makes sure that the balcony catches every breath of breeze on a hot and humid day. White is a predominant feature of the condo, both inside and out, where the raw concrete of the walls and terrace floor turn to a bleached white in the dazzle of the morning sun.

right: The outside walls of the apartment are punctuated by floor-to-ceiling glass doors that give access from the dining room and master bedroom. The balcony faces east on one side, and north on the other, so sun floods the apartment all day.

night vision

If the views from the condo are spectacular during the day, by night the world outside is transformed into a magical *son et lumière*, where the traffic streaming on South Bridge toward the high-rise apartments across the Bay becomes a flow of constantly changing light and sound.

The espresso-colored leather-look porcelain tiles on the floor provide a dark base note, above which the white walls take on a glowing luminosity against the backdrop of midnight blue outside. The owner loves the rough grain of bare concrete, which most people would disguise with a covering of stucco or plaster, and insisted on leaving it raw

below: White walls, curtains, and furniture pick up the glow from the subtle and layered lighting, and seem to get brighter as the darkness outside deepens. The only color in the living area is provided by the floral rug, which is lit by the star lights arranged in a rectangle above.

below left: The high dining table, designed by the owner, is made from a slab of green Irish marble supported on tubular steel with oversized castors. Set for supper, the table is perfectly positioned for a view of the Bay at night.

below right: The contemporary white leather sofa, from Edra, curves round the end of the living room, and has an adjustable seat back that gives it maximum flexibility. The soft white leather assumes a sheen at night, lit from above by the Flos lamp.

on all the ceilings. Leaving the structure of the building so exposed means that instaling recessed lighting is out of the equation, so low-voltage mini lights, suspended from wires, have been strung across the ceiling. The effect at night is of a grid of tiny star lights that project pools of soft light onto the floor but don't detract attention from the view outside. Supplementing the ambience of the ceiling lights, a tall contemporary floor lamp provides task lighting for reading, and a row of pendants over the dining table supplies a soft glow for an evening supper with friends.

cutting edge

It's little wonder that pale blue and white are such a popular combination for bedrooms. It's a pairing that reflects the blue sky and white clouds of the great outdoors. Relaxing and soothing, the tranquility of nature is harnessed to bring serenity to a city dweller. When you live in a high-rise apartment overlooking the water, sky, sea, and clouds are part of your everyday experience, and bringing the outside in seems as natural as breathing. The same effect can be applied to a less elevated living situation. A small, dark space will always respond to the airiness that soft shades of blue will bring, and painting any room white immediately expands the space. Archeologists have discovered fragments of blue and white in ancient Roman frescoes, and the same can be found in almost every period of history, but the charm of blue and white continues to appeal and can be found at the forefront of cutting edge design.

With high ceilings and a wall of glass, the master bedroom of this Miami condo relies on white for the walls and drapes, and the frost-blue quilt gently undulates in front of the outstanding view. The sheen of the fabric is echoed in the impressive chandelier suspended from the concrete ceiling, reflecting every variation of texture around it.

top left: With a brilliant take on the classic glass chandelier, the designer of this Light Shade Shade, from Moooi, has wrapped a traditional set of crystal drops in a metallized plastic outer skin. The raw concrete ceiling is replicated in the surface in the daytime, but turned on at night the chandelier appears in its original state.

left: The view across the causeway to the Art Deco District is breathtaking by day and night, and the colors of the water and sky have informed the choice of accessories.

right: Waking up to the morning sun sparkling across the waters of the Bay, there's a sense that high-rise life in Miami offers the best of both worlds; the buzz of city living combined with the delights of wide open spaces.

sun and shadows

The landscape in and around the city of Cape Town, South Africa, is widely diverse. Within only a few miles—or even a few minutes—of the city, soft, white sandy beaches, verdant forests, and spectacular mountain views can all be experienced. With such a divergent setting, it's not surprising that the architectural styles of the city vary so extensively, too. From low, whitewashed cottages on the dunes, to modernist apartments in the city, from Cape Cod-style wooden houses to Colonial Classical buildings and the sprawling individuality of the townships, Cape Town, also known as "The Mother City," is a cosmopolitan and animated place to live.

above: A pair of glass doors can be thrown open to allow a summer breeze to cool the interior of the glass-walled living room. The colors of the garden are invited inside, and thrown into relief by the underlying white of the carpet and floor tiles.

above: A wall inside the house is painted a fearless, uncompromising orange that makes a striking contrast to the vivid blue of the unclouded summer sky.

above right: The dramatically rounded walls of glass and steel are perhaps best seen from the garden. The tiled terrace is shaded all day by the tall indigenous trees and the sleek curves of the sun deck echo the smooth, space-age shapes of the main building.

On the lush green slopes of Constantia, the extraordinary house called "Falcon's Eye" has marvellous views across the tree tops to faraway mountains. The house is a circular glass and steel building that radiates outward from a central hub. The main living area sits within an entire wall of curved glass, whose white floor becomes a magic lantern show of dancing shadows as the brilliant African sunshine filters through the branches of the sheltering trees. The high glass walls allow unimpeded views of the sky, not by any means always blue. The mountain-side location means that low clouds can sit around all morning until the heat of the sun dispels them by noon.

From the white-stained boards of the sun deck, you can gaze out over lush palms to the far horizon with miles of uninterrupted landscape and the Hottentot mountains across False Bay. It's a bird's eye view and here the owners have taken full advantage of the house's position on the slopes by utilizing the roof of the bedrooms below to make a stunning first-floor terrace.

The curved edges of the decking describe an arc that is bordered by fine, tubular steel railings, giving some degree of protection without blocking the view. Reflective and simple, white makes a perfect foil for

below: As gentle as the curve on a bird's wing, the undulating shapes of these aluminum sun loungers laze in the sun and face the far horizon.

below right: The narrow tubular legs of the contemporary "Venus" stools resonate with the steel railings that run round the perimeter of the deck. The long narrow bar makes an excellent place to sip a cocktail after dark with the lights of the city twinkling below.

below: Radiating lines of the narrow decking planks contrast with the broad sweeping curves that form the outline of the terrace. It's a strong combination underlining the boldly-drawn curvature that epitomizes the spirit of the house.

the heat and light, and the rigorous simplicity of the aluminum sun loungers demands that the materials used are of the finest quality. Wooden decking comes in many guises, and natural hardwoods, like teak or ipe, will weather to a very attractive pale gray over time if left unoiled, but the process of whitening the wood can be hastened if it is stained with a pale wood stain. To do it yourself, choose a stain that has been specially formulated for outdoors and remember that a dry deck will absorb the stain best. Pick a cloudy day for the job, as hot sun tends to separate the ingredients and dry them prematurely.

summer whites

When you have views this spectacular, who needs anything but white? It's the philosophy behind the Zen-like interior of Boutique Manolo, a small luxury hotel that nestles into the side of Signal Hill, only minutes away from central Cape Town, and with superb views over Table Mountain. When the owners, a pair of Dutch restaurateurs, decided to change direction and open an exclusive hotel, they found a small modern house in Tamboerskloof set over four floors, and extended it on both sides to arrive at a building large enough for four guest suites and a penthouse apartment. In the penthouse, the living room relies on a combination of textures to bring comfort and luxury to the understated scheme; the sheen on pale leather, a sumptuous white, deep-pile rug, slatted American shutters, and the gentle flutter of soft voile curtains at the open doors.

left: Light bounces off the edges of reflective surfaces and brings a depth of shadow to the white matt textures of the suede-look pillows and deep-pile woolen rug.

right: Bang in the center of the living room, the metallic globe of a vase recreates the white walls and furniture that is seen in the depths of its reflective surface.

Early morning in the hills above Cape Town, and the sun hasn't yet burned off the mist and cloud that soften the horizon. The tiny outdoor terrace that leads off the penthouse living room is bordered with panels of clear safety glass that protect guests from falling, but are almost totally invisible. To sit on the white canvas-covered sofas, taking coffee and a pastry before the sun gets too hot, is to feel as if you are flying above the waking city.

White is the ideal foil to the dark, woven garden furniture, and although white canvas may initially seem an impractical fabric for seat covers, prone to stains from coffee, newspaper print, and jam, in fact it's one of the easiest to keep clean. Removed and laundered in the washing machine on a hot wash, stains can be boiled out and the covers restored to their pristine snowiness.

left: The cushions of outdoor seats need to be brought inside when it rains, and kept spotlessly clean if they are to stay white. Alternatively, if made from a waterproof fabric like Sunbrella, they can stay out whatever the weather.

right: Seen from the top floor, the spotless white paving, pocket handkerchief-sized green lawn, and unusual red lap pool look immaculate and neatly drawn in the geometrically-designed garden below.

The owners of Boutique Manolo came up with the revolutionary idea of painting their tiny lap pool red instead of the more customary blue. It's a startling color to see as one descends the steep steps from the top of the house, down through the lush Mediterranean gardens for a cool bathe, but one which reflects the ultra-modern styling of the house with its chic, all-white interior stamped with red.

The owners have designed the hotel with a view to relaxation and luxury in all its aspects, and the unspoiled brilliance of the white stucco surround of the pool area keeps the retreat one step ahead of its competitors. Pure white outdoor areas need to be swept and washed every morning and the swimming pool diligently netted for stray leaves, but it's worth the effort to see the effect of pure white against the deep red of the water. Positioned on the steep hillside, and shaded by trees at some point all through the day, the pool and terrace are popular resting spots for guests who come to Manolo for a welcome and undisturbed break. The city is only moments away, but the peace and tranquility are undisturbed.

right: Four poolside loungers are covered with stretch terry toweling covers that can be removed each evening for washing, and the red towels, rolled and ready for each guest, provide a contrasting splash of color.

below: Although one or two guests have hesitated to descend into the pool because of the vivid red color, they have been reassured that it's only the walls that have been colored, not the water.

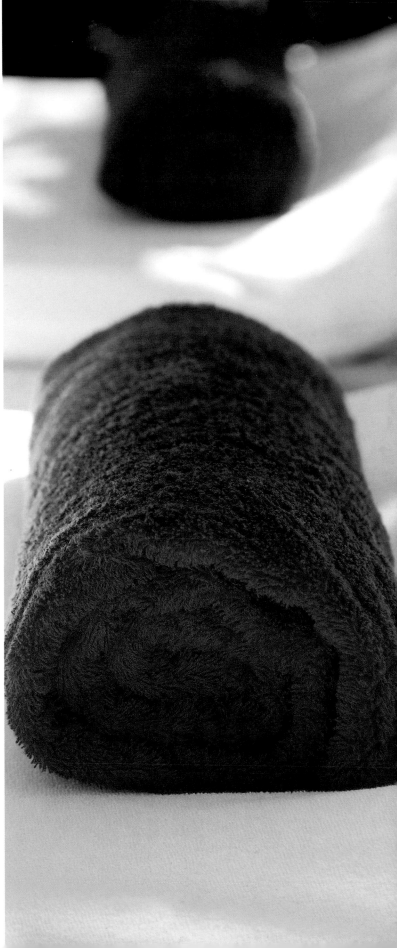

left: It's a steep climb to the top of the house up the white concrete steps, but the way is made easier by the shade afforded by the garden planting and there are plenty of interesting spots to pause at on the way.

far right: All the windows in the guest suites are screened by long white voile drapes that can be pulled across to keep the rooms private and cool.

below: A tank of white and gold koi carp is cunningly set into the space beside the steps. Their glass-fronted home makes an ever-changing and compelling sight as guests wend their way from a dip in the pool.

outdoor cool

Although not big enough for their needs, when this narrow house was first viewed by Peter Zeeuw and Leen Filius, they soon realized that the tall, 1970s building had the potential to be transformed into a contemporary and stunning retreat. The dramatic outlook was certainly one of its best features, and it took two years of hard work to redesign the whole of the interior, and to change the levels of the garden with its stunning tank of koi carp.

The outside of the house is gleaming white from top to bottom, with floor-to-ceiling glass doors that open onto private balconies and four floors negotiated by means of a series of steep, white concrete steps and spiral staircases. Seen against the vivid blue of the sky, the house has an international look that could place it anywhere in the world, from Monte Carlo to Sydney, and as the sun travels across the sky, strong diagonal shadows are seen making their slow progress across the terraces. The garden plays an essential part in the external environment as the strong horizontals and verticals of the building are softened and cooled by the rich planting that tumbles down the hillside. In the early morning after the sprinkler has finished its work, the lower part of the garden, still in shade, is a deliciously refreshing and cool haven from which to emerge into the heat.

When temperatures soar and the sky is blue, living outside is pure heaven, and it's always a joy to eat outside, from the first sip of juice in the morning to the last coffee of the evening. But there have to be compromises and ways to keep the area cool. It's necessary to have plenty of shade from the sun and to find ways of letting breezes cool the spaces if your outside dining room is not to become uncomfortably hot. White is ideal for an indoor-outdoor room when every surface becomes dazzlingly pure and reflective.

At Boutique Manolo, the front gate from the road outside opens into an inner courtyard furnished with two oversized slatted daybeds designed by Peter Zeeuw and made locally. Breakfast is taken under the

below left: A spiral staircase winds its way up to the kitchen from a lower floor. Painted gray against the white of the floor and walls, the stairs are made more negotiable by the contrast.

below: Soft canvas pillows are plumped up on the daybed, and the slatted backs add a touch of texture against the plain white wall behind.

below: An open window in the kitchen catches the breeze on the high mountain side. Open doors funnel the breeze into the courtyard, cooling the air with a gentle movement.

enormous white parasols that shade the whole of the courtyard, forming a canvas roof that can easily be taken down when they are not needed. Coffee is prepared and eggs cooked in the minimal, contemporary kitchen whose long windows overlook the view at the back, shaded by slender Venetian blinds.

A sleek set of sliding glass doors folds completely back and transforms the kitchen into a spacious outside room in summer, giving the effect of a single room that breaks down all notions of inside or outside. Although the glass doors are so unobtrusive in summer, they can be closed during winter months when, by contrast, the typical Cape Town winter is chilly and often wet.

chapter three

seaside whites

beach life

On the long sandy beaches of the Cape Pensinsula, 20 miles south of Cape Town, the South African village of Kommetjie is a haven of white thatched cottages that sit snugly behind the sand dunes, protected by a range of mountain peaks, and looking out at the blue Atlantic. This guest house is a typical example of the early Cape Dutch style, with white walls both inside and out and a traditional thatched roof designed to keep the rooms below cool and shaded. Guests are encouraged to feel completely at home, and white is used throughout the house on walls, furniture, curtains, and covers, to create a pure, cool environment.

above: The pale blue woodwork of Sunset Beach Guest House gives the simple vernacular style a fresh and contemporary look against the white walls.

right: The white flagstone terrace at the back of the house has spectacular views of the mountains and beach. Guests relax on white-covered sun loungers after a cold dip in the sea, just a stone's throw from the house.

A blue-and-white bedroom must be one of the coolest schemes possible, and under the vividness of the South African sun the purity and freshness of the combination is a pleasure from the first light of day. Pure, white-painted walls are teamed with a set of sheer white muslin drapes at the windows that catch every waft of sea-scented air. A set of crisp white bed linen is de rigeur for a seaside house, and white accessories, like lampshades, painted wooden bed heads, and picture frames, add texture to the two-toned scheme.

Of course it's the sea outside the windows that is the big draw, and introducing a flash of blue to the interior helps bring the outside in and creates a fresh coastal ambience. The prospect outside the windows is a constantly changing scene of azure and cerulean, sapphire and indigo. Calm and blue on a still day, or wild and gray when the wind blows, the scene is an ever-changing delight, and an interior works best when it underlines, rather than competes with, the beauties of nature.

left: Each one of the five bedrooms at Sunset Beach has a sea view, and part of the experience is waking up each morning to look out of the double doors that open onto the dunes and the ocean beyond.

right: Blue-and-white gingham is the obvious choice for a country-style bedroom. It's a look that has all the simplicity you want for a seaside home, but one that has been warmed with the natural colors of the thatched roof.

The first European-style houses to be built in the Cape Town area were constructed by the settlers of the Dutch East India Company in the mid to late seventeenth century. These settlers colonized the watered valleys of the Eastern Cape and built low, whitewashed cottages with thatched roofs. These early houses were purely utilitarian, consisting of three rooms with a steeply pitched roof supported by timbers, and were given thick, plastered walls as a protection against the summer heat. As the settlers became more prosperous, a central gable was often added, which resulted in the typically beautiful "Cape Dutch" style. It is a style that has its roots in Medieval Europe and the islands of Indonesia.

In country areas there are still some beautiful examples of the early vernacular houses and the simple, highly practical design is a building style that is often used today. Many of the beach homes at Kommetjie have been built with the same white-washed walls and thatched roofs, and some are extended from the coastal whaler's cottages of the nineteenth century. African thatching has been used for centuries to keep houses cool in summer and warm in winter, and modern versions are often made using a combination of thatching grass and a superior reed, known as Cape Reed, which is less dust-retentive and ideal on the inside layer of the roof.

left: The steeply-pitched roof at Sunset Beach Guest House is seen sweeping down to the corner of the all-white landing. The newly-thatched roof has an evocative smell when it is first instaled, a smell rich in the scent of the ocean and one which recalls its natural origin.

below: A tiny ensuite bathroom has been decorated with typical, seaside-style tongue-and-groove boarding and painted in a brilliant white. It is only the inside of the thatch that reminds us that we are in Africa.

dining at dusk

left: As the sun sets over the sea, guests at Sunset Beach are treated to an evening meal on the terrace, with the spectacle of the glowing evening sky over the mountains as it sinks into darkness.

below right: Polished glass, gleaming china, and spotless white linen are classic ingredients for a table setting. Laid for two under the night sky, it's a setting that can't fail to effortlessly impress.

below: Flowers for a table setting are often best kept small and unobtrusive. Papery white flowers picked from the natural Fynbos garden in early October fill a pair of tiny glasses at each place.

In a climate where it's too hot to eat outside in the daytime, setting a table under the stars is a practical way to dine and even the simplest meal will take on a romantic aura. A white tablecloth, china, and napkins make sure that any residual light is reflected, and glasses and silver cutlery will sparkle in the shadows. As dusk deepens, light up an outdoor table with a variety of candles that will add their own particular ambience to the meal. If the evening is still enough for a naked flame to survive, use citronella candles; their lemon-scented vapor will repel mosquitoes and midges. If there's any chance of a breeze, a set of contemporary-style lanterns will give protection to the fragile flames.

weekend haven

Beach houses at Grayton Beach, in Florida, can be subjected to destructive tides and ferocious gale-force winds. Architect Carey McWhorter was commissioned to design a contemporary weekend house that would make the most of the amazing views, while at the same time keeping it safe from nature's excesses. The living areas and bedrooms were raised high above the dunes, supported on pale concrete pillars that give them security from high tides, and giving the first floor deck a unique vantage point. Sunny and hot in the day, the terrace faces the setting sun, and spectacular sunsets are seen most evenings.

left: As the afternoon progresses, a row of white-painted, wooden Adirondack chairs are lined up along the bleached deck for the nightly ritual of watching the sun go down. The unrelieved purity of the white deck is given vivacity with deliciously colored accessories.

below: In the middle of summer, visitors and family take refuge from the noon heat by resting in the air-conditioned interior. The floor-to-ceiling windows are shaded by white mesh blinds that reduce the glare from the sun, but the glorious view is unobstructed.

vibrant hues

The white interior of the beach house, designed to feel cool and serene even on the hottest of days, is enlivened with flashes of vivid color that create dramatic pools of brilliance and reflect the natural world seen outside the windows. The azure of the sea and sky at midday and the glowing green of the swaying grasses in the dunes are echoed in the color of the floor-length curtains of the master bedroom. The wall-to-wall curtains can be drawn back to allow a full view of the beach from the bed, and the sliding doors are opened at night to let in the soporific sound of the crashing surf that soothes visitors to sleep.

It is only in a climate where the sunlight is strong and sharp that the combination of brilliant white and bright color has maximum impact. Chosen for a room with a soft, northern light, this intensity of color would look harsh and overpowering. In a sunny southern house, however, the brightness of the natural light is met by the sparkling white of the walls and bed linen, and the concentrated hues of the paint and fabric seem undiluted and fresh.

left: The clean lines of the modern architecture, with its pared-back detailing and simplicity of design, is emphasized by the blocks of color provided by the two-tone curtains. It's a combination that ensures the drama outside the window is seen to full advantage.

right: Snaking up the wall above the steps that lead to the bedroom, the metal hand rail has been painted in the same brilliant blue as the curtains, and provides a bright contrast to the white of the walls.

outdoor color

Raised up on strengthened concrete pillars, the living and sleeping areas of the house are high enough to catch the full beauty of the view, while being elevated away from flooding. The shady areas underneath the building have been given a creative flamboyance that steers them away from utilitarianism and brings a *joie de vivre* to the pallid concrete of the structure. It's an approach that characterizes the entire house, and one which brings humor and a celebratory feel fitting to a building whose sole purpose is to relax and revive its visitors.

below: A small swimming pool has been tucked into the space between the columns under the house. A more conventional designer would have been satisfied with the blue pool, but here, a pink-painted pillar rises out of the blue water and a painted chair adds a splash of sunshine yellow.

right: A pair of cold outdoor showers stands waiting for sandy bathers as they reach the house from the dunes and beach. With another touch of wit and color, the white concrete recess around the showers has been painted in a vivid shade of pink.

bauhaus inspired

The modernist architectural style inspired by Bauhaus architects Mies van der Rohe and Walter Gropius in the 1940s took root in Florida after the Second World War, and became known as the Sarasota School. Florida-born architect Carey McWhorter acknowledges that he has been influenced by these design principles since his student days in New York and Atlanta, and he used the pared-back, modernist approach when commissioned to build this contemporary beach house in Destin, Florida. His brief was to design an open-plan home with glass walls that would take full advantage of the panoramic views of the Gulf of Mexico and that would harmonize with the pure white sand from which it rises.

right: The house glows when viewed from the dunes after sundown, but local regulations permit only low-level exterior lights. Hatching sea turtles emerge at night from the white quartz sand from July to October and make their way to the sea, attracted by the lightest open area.

below: The white stucco finish on the concrete blocks contrasts with the floor-to-ceiling glass windows typical of this Floridian style of architecture. Seen at dusk as the light falls, the house is a beacon of simplicity and understated beauty on this part of the coastline.

Although the white-stucco sun decks on the first and second floors are perfect for watching the ocean, depending on the angle of the sun the overhanging roof terraces provide welcome shade at all times. The architect has used the configuration of the necessary structure to build areas that are always shady and help keep the interior of the house cool. The ground-floor pool, situated between supporting pillars, makes sure that weekenders and vacationers have a place to cool off when the sea is rough and strong currents make it unsafe to bathe. "Environmental modernism" is how this architectural style has been labeled, and the house is a perfect example of how the architect has worked within the strictures of nature.

left: The dazzling white sand and the perfect azure of the Gulf of Mexico create one of the purest views in the natural world, and the pared-back structure of the first floor deck has no extraneous detailing to distract a nature-watcher.

below: The white concrete pillars were sunk 30 feet deep into the soft sand of the beach before the house was built. The strong verticals and horizontals create a canopy over the blue pool.

retro style

Although this house is completely contemporary, finished in 2005, the underlying influence of the building is of the post-war 1950s with its experimental use of angular shapes and cuboid blocks. Libby Sims-Patrick, the Atlanta-based interior designer who devised the furnishings and color choices, has worked creatively within the stylistic remit. Without turning the interior into a retro museum piece, she has introduced elements of color and furniture styles that underline the historic stimulus of the house. The rooms and terraces glow with plenty of white balanced by accents of color, and the furniture is practical and family-friendly while at the same time looking stylishly modern.

left: Flashes of color enliven a tiny top terrace that has been constructed with polished concrete and horizontally-grooved wood. The citrus shades of the pillows and the aqua side table belong to an essentially 1950s palette that perfectly complement the roots of the house's design history.

right: The circular skylight allows a view of the blue sky above, and daylight illuminates the whole area in the complex play of light and shadow that is always seen to best advantage in an all-white environment.

Nature is the all-important element in any beach-front home, and ocean and sky take center stage in every room in the house. Florida is known as the "sunshine state" where the sun shines for two-thirds of all possible daylight hours and is characterized by long, hot, humid summers. In this climate it's necessary to keep the interiors of beach homes cool and shady to provide a refuge from the sun.

A white interior serves this purpose best, and the architect and interior designer have collaborated to bring together a fusion of simple lines and statement pieces that give an unhurried, timeless flavor. Curtains and blinds are negligible, either non-existent, as here, or of the most understated variety. They are used simply to shade a room from the heat or to keep out early morning daylight in the bedrooms, and neither impede nor distract from the view. In the living area, the walls and woodwork are all white, while gray and white carpet tiles make an effective and stylish covering for the white polished concrete floor.

left: In the white and glass living room on the first floor, the view is open and magnificent, and the red "Pop Chair" and footstool make a strikingly colorful accent against the blue and white scene beyond.

top right: A corner angle of one of the roof terraces, seen from below, has an echo of an ocean liner as it stands sentinel over the ever-moving ocean.

right: On the exterior, the strong horizontal and vertical lines of the building have a resonance with the flat landscape of North Florida and the white stucco makes a dramatic impact against the floating clouds and summer blue skies.

contemporary monochrome

Black and white is a timeless combination, and there can be no better situation for teaming the two than in the kitchen. Pure white worktops made from modern materials look minimal and contemporary, are hygienic and heat resistant, and can be molded to form seam-free countertops with an integral sink that allows no place for bacteria to hide. Glossy black cabinets that contrast with the gleaming white of the worktops and walls make the perfect solution for the kitchen of this contemporary, architect-designed beach house, where the understated design allows the view to be paramount. Dramatic blue glass light fittings illuminate the eating area, and visually bring down the height of the ceilings.

Like many schemes that have been designed using just two basic colors, a black-and-white room will always benefit from the introduction of flashes of contrasting bright color. The strong blue of the lights is a fixture, but a vase of brilliant red roses and a bowl of bright green grapes add an extra dimension. Here, as in so many of the rooms in this summer house, it's the view outside that predominates, and the simplicity of the kitchen, with its windows on two sides, means that cooks and diners can easily stay in contact with nature.

left: The central breakfast bar, made of the same white material as the worktops, is raised up on steel plinths to give a view of the sea for anyone sitting down to eat.

below: In midsummer, air conditioning can struggle to keep up with rising temperatures, so mesh blinds help the kitchen stay comfortable. Gray-painted concrete floors run throughout all the communal areas and are an initiative to keep bare feet pleasantly cool.

Summertime in Florida demands a way of life that goes with the weather conditions, and eating outside is not always an option during the hottest time of day. Families may prefer to eat inside, where the air is cool and air-conditioned, and eating areas are designed accordingly. In this house, the spectacular views are guaranteed by plate glass windows that are wrapped around the living areas of the house allowing the outlook to be unhindered throughout mealtimes, and furniture is positioned in the best possible location. The black-and-white theme has been carried through from the kitchen, and the dining area has a similar graphic, contemporary feel. The understated black wooden tabletop is mounted on a steel frame, and the white molded chairs make a sleek and unobtrusive set in the predominantly white room. Contrasting color accents have been added with the red and aqua china that links the table setting with the reclining chair nearby.

left: Creative place settings only need a little imagination to bring style and flair to a monochrome dining room. Woven place mats add a natural note, and the mixed colours of red, black, and blue plates and bowls are layered at each setting. A fresh chili pepper is placed inside each bowl for a splash of hot red.

right: The dining table is set for an informal family supper, and a row of glass pendant lights add light, not color, along the table at night. Empty wine glasses each have a tea light inside; an idea that would be useful in an outdoor setting on an evening with a light breeze.

using color

One way of brightening up a small room is to paint a feature wall with color and decorate all other surfaces in brilliant white. It's a wonderful way of balancing strong sunlight, and gives character and impact to square rooms that might otherwise look a little bland. It's a technique that works well in small bedrooms and bathrooms where space is restricted. In this contemporary house with its roof terraces and large windows, the views at the front are simply stunning and the living areas facing the beach need no extra decorative effects. But in rooms on the side of the house, the outlook is less prepossessing. To deflect from the view of neighboring houses and to keep the hot sunlight out, the tall windows are screened with Roman blinds and the walls filled with strong Mediterranean color to compensate.

right: A small guest bedroom and en-suite shower room are given a piquant shot of color with tangerine and lime. The two shades have the same tonal quality that enables them to sit comfortably together and are edged with brisk white woodwork.

below left: A tiny shower room was given plenty of style when the facing wall was washed with a sharp, tangy splash of color. The black cupboards and white worktop sharpen up the color.

below: The interior designer has kept a sense of continuity throughout the house with recurring shapes and themes. The circular mirror in a nearby shower room is seen again in the round panel above the bed, painted with easy swirls of complementary grays and blues on white.

It's well worth familiarizing yourself with basic color theory before using color with as strong an impact as in this bedroom. The principles are simple, but without a little basic knowledge of how colors relate, it can be frustrating finding shades that blend harmoniously.

An easy way to see how color works is to look at a color wheel, where the three primary colors—red, yellow, and blue—are arranged around a circle. Each one of the primaries can be mixed with its neighbor, so red and blue blend to make purple, blue and yellow create green, and yellow and red mixed together make orange—the three secondary colors. Arranged in a wheel, the shades blend seamlessly from one to another, each color

changing its character as it's mixed with more and more of its neighbor. The value of the color wheel is that arranged in this way the colors opposite one another, called complementary colors, can be understood and used in combinations that give a spark to each, an effect often employed by interior designers. Orange and blue, purple and yellow, red and green—all are complementary colors. The secret lies in using just a touch of the opposite color to add an accent which brings life and verve to a scheme. The brightness of the light is another factor, and only rooms with plenty of natural sunlight can afford to use color this vivid.

left: The effect of a whole wall of orange is startling. But the secret lies in the way it has been used with restraint. The color itself is toned down with white—it's a warm tangerine not hot orange, and the neutral carpet, white paintwork, and furniture keep the look cool. The black-and-white painting holds the color back too, balancing it with a monochrome image.

right: The blue accessories are an example of how complementary color can be skilfully introduced to cool down a hot color, although it is the sea outside the private balcony that is the major accent. Apart from the single feature wall, the room has been painted in brilliant white.

When deciding on a paint shade for an entire room or for just a feature wall, never choose from the paint manufacturer's shade card alone. The amount of color shown is too small, and color changes drastically depending on the available light. Make a selection of three shades that you like, and buy small sample pots, then paint a large sheet of card with each. The cards can be held in place while you observe the different colors in situ. Remember that the greater the expanse of color, the deeper it will appear, so it's worth always picking colors a tone lighter than you finally want. Hold the cards up to walls all round the room, and see how different light affects the color. Bright sun will bleach out the color, whereas on a shaded wall color always appears denser.

far left: Adjacent to a blue and white bedroom, an en-suite bathroom has a deep alcove holding a Roman-style bath. The blue mosaic tiling gives the bath the inviting feel of a tiny indoor pool sunk into the floor of the white curved bay.

left: The wall of windows lets in a huge amount of sunlight, and curtains are necessary to help keep early morning light out. Long white canvas curtains—the style often found in a hospital ward—are hung across the window walls.

right: Outside the tall windows of this second-storey bedroom, the ocean sparkles in brilliant blue hues. Breakers foam onto the white sand and the sky is often scudding with white clouds. The designer has picked up on the hues of nature to combine brilliant white with a feature wall of sky blue, but it is the vivid shot of complementary orange that gives life to the cool combination.

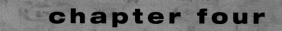

chapter four

textural whites

moroccan influences

Here in summer, life revolves around the outdoor terraces and swimming pool with swimming parties and barbecues—called braais in South Africa. The rough-plastered brick wall at the end of the seating area has been formed into a series of rounded arches, giving the terrace a distinctly Moroccan flavor.

The bench wraps around the corner to form a sheltered spot for sitting out of the Cape Town wind which can blow hard, even in summer. Roughly rendered with natural plaster, the outline of the bricks shows beneath a surface that has become mottled over time. Adding to the textures, the benches and daybed were constructed from blocks and plastered with white stucco which has developed a series of fine cracks in its polished surface over the years. It's a traditional method of building seen all over the world, simple and unsophisticated, but with an authenticity of materials that makes it a frequently used technique even in the most stylish and contemporary of modern buildings.

left: Found in the souk in Marrakech, a battered wooden lantern adds another dimension to the textures in the seating corner, and one that harmonizes with the white metal wall plaque on the wall above.

right: Shaded by a large white parasol, the corner is comfortably out of the sun, whether it's used for morning coffee or an afternoon nap. The rusting metal table adds yet another texture to the melée.

farmhouse chic

Predominantly white, with the only touch of color introduced in the form of an ethnic, woven kelim, the living room of this farmhouse near Yserfontein, South Africa, has been finished with a variety of creamy whites and a multiplicity of texture. The owners of "Inglenook" have taken a pragmatic approach and built the house with the simplest of materials that each have their own inherent texture—the sheen of steel girders and corrugated sheet metal, the unfinished quality of painted brick pillars, a floor of polished concrete, and the transparency of glass. The structure throughout is pared-back and minimal with no frills or expensive finishes.

Furniture is of the simplest style, too. A pair of crunchy linen-covered sofas and a roughly-hewn wooden bench, serving as a coffee table, stand in front of an antique chair imported after a vacation in Indonesia. What gives the room distinction and a truly individual style is the confident use of the carved wooden panel from Bali that has been set into the wall above the window, and the crystal chandelier that hangs from the roof.

left: The roof has a deep overhang at the side of the house that creates shade for the living room and a covered walkway that runs the full length of the house.

above right: The combination of a low-cost, industrial building material like corrugated metal, used to enable rain to drain quickly and easily from the roof, and the glamour of a glittering chandelier is a witty and delightful departure from the norm.

weathered wood

Eating al fresco with friends and family is a traditional vacation activity, and it's always worth choosing a spot that's out of the wind and shaded from the sun. A place under an overhanging roof, a canvas awning, or a covered loggia all make marvelous places to sit and linger after lunch, but there's nothing quite like the dappled shade and shifting shadows that a leafy tree will provide. Find a salvaged set of garden furniture with an aged patina, or buy new teak garden furniture from a sustainable source that will fade to a wonderfully pale, silvery gray if it's left out in the sun and rain for a couple of seasons. Without oiling, the wood will develop fine cracks in its surface, but these don't damage the wood, and only add to the weathered texture. This table still has fragments of its original finish, which is slowly disappearing as the elements do their work and the surface assumes a silvery patina.

above left: An antique birdcage from Goa, in India, sits under the base of the tree. The fretwork of wire and aged wood seen against the grain of the tree bark provides a still life of texture and shadows.

left: A loaf of country bread, salad, and a plate of fresh tomatoes make a colorful and simple lunch. The African-inspired plates emulate a technique called "sgraffito," in which a pattern is scratched into the dark glaze, revealing the white clay body underneath.

right: The table and chairs are placed under the shade of an old Mimosa tree, and the white gravel underfoot adds another crunchy texture to the scene.

bare essentials

The owners of the house made no attempt to hide the inherent structure of the building when they designed the house with the help of architect Anthony Tulleken. The original concept was for a "barn-meets-warehouse," which explains the emphasis on raw materials and the non-domestic style of the interior. The bare bones are raw and uncompromising, an approach that resonates with the landscape outside—25 acres of pristine South African Fynbos (Afrikaans for fine bush). In the lofty central hallway, light gleams along the white polished concrete floor into the bathroom beyond, where a white basin and molded mirror frame glimmer against the slate walls. Luminous light from the high windows moves across the natural brick walls as the sun travels round the house, emphasizing the height of the roof that helps keep the house cool. The somber quality of bare brick and slate, the dark wood of the door frames, the African sculptures on the walls, and the antique chest form a subdued backdrop to the brilliance of the flashes of white and the bar of sunlight.

left: A whimsical light fitting finds a golden cherub flying through the air with two crystal drops, a capricious touch that's in joyful contrast to the workaday style of the hall with its bare brick and concrete.

right: Only just seen from the hallway, the copper tube that has been made into a utilitarian faucet makes another quirky feature, juxtaposed as it is with the white-painted mirror frame that was found in a Cape Town antique shop.

left: White concrete stairs rise up from the polished floor below, the smooth planes of the treads catching the light and creating layers of texture against the brick of the hall and the fabulously gnarled handrail.

right: The contorted contours of the handrail are actually a few lengths of dry jungle vine that twists as it dries. They were brought back from a vacation in Sumatra and bound together to form the handrail.

The house is filled with a highly original use of materials and textures, and the juxtaposition of ethnic artefacts and more sophisticated objects makes a walk through the rooms an adventure of discovery as each door is thrown open. On the ground floor, the bathroom resembles the interior of a cave. The back wall has been given a fabulous covering of slate pieces, fixed into the plaster in horizontal layers, and as the afternoon sun slants through the blinds, the colors of the slate, which came from Paarl, on the Western Cape, glow and change with the shifting light. The texture is made to look even more rich and multi-faceted by the smoothness of the white bath and the stuccoed surround.

left: The walls and floor of the walk-in shower are finished with pale, plaster-colored stucco and the glass shower screen fits into a base of recycled wood. The tones of the walls are dappled and soft, and the paneled door from Java adds a further dimension of texture.

right: Two contemporary white vases make idiosyncratic shapes against the rough hewn slate wall, lighting up the corner as they catch the light.

simple elements

A strong distinction of texture and tone stages a theatrical effect in the bathroom that leads to the master bedroom. The pale wall has a plaster finish and acts as a divider between the two rooms, as well as a support for the shower. The wall is softly polished with a smoothness that has a gentle, sensual quality, but the dark wood of the carved screen, with its fretwork panels, is heavy and pierced with light. It's the union of the two that brings out the characteristic attribute of each and both have a bigger impact because of it.

left: The rustic shower is simple and charming with its copper pipes and plumber's merchant fixings. The design is perfect for the mix of farmhouse and industrial building that the owners and architect had in mind.

right: Dividing walls can sometimes create obsolete areas, but in the master bedroom the open layout of the space allows a flow of air through the rooms that is badly needed on hot nights in the South African bush.

coconut grove

Set in a one-acre garden of tropical density that could easily convince a visitor they are deep in the jungles of South-east Asia, architect Max Strang has built a unique home for his family in Coconut Grove, only a few miles from the tower blocks of downtown Miami, Florida. The house is long and narrow and has for its inspiration both the modernist work of the Florida Sarasota School of Architecture and the spirit of a traditional Indonesian long house. Strang grew up in a house designed by Gene Leedy, one of the founding fathers of the Bauhaus-inspired Sarasota School, and his own house, built with a grid of steel girders and faced with pale oolite limestone, features many of the same elements.

left: The design is edgy and experimental, and the house nestles into the surrounding palm fronds and banana leaves, supporting the environmental-modernist approach of landscape enhancing the character of a building.

right: The small cottage that originally stood on the site has left its mark. The Strangs used the footprint of the foundations to build the complex of pools, which include a lap pool and a hot tub. Around the pools, white fossilized coral reef, or Florida keystone, delineates the edges with a deeply-grained finish.

balinese lifestyle

The first-floor terrace is open to the elements and sits high among the surrounding banana palms and bamboos, making a marvellous chill-out zone for humid summer living. The wooden decking, made of ipe, a sustainable hardwood from Indonesia, drains easily after one of the torrential downpours that characterize the Miami weather patterns. For eight months of the year outdoor living is a necessity, and one of the three central "pods," paneled with marine ply and painted white, houses the summer kitchen. A buying trip to Indonesia furnished the terrace with woven banana-leaf sofas and the wealth of natural textures only serves to reinforce the interchange between nature and design.

below: With tiny lizards that run across the wooden decking of the terrace and the birds that flit through the trees at eye level, it's clear that the environment is very much part of the mix.

right: Found in the garden of the original 1920s cottage where the family lived for two years while the house was being built, a rusty bath tub is filled with iced water and used to cool beer and champagne for parties—or simply for washing the dogs.

below: White paneling and pure white seat pillows bring a luminosity to the natural textures and shade of the terrace. The areas of white reflect light, without which the area could look dark and somber.

Reclaimed teak, antique benches, palm trunk vases, and modern Balinese carvings—all these have found a natural place on the open-air terrace and throughout the rest of the house. The Strangs took a buying trip to Bali in 2005, where they sourced both new and antique furniture and artefacts, hiring a container to ship them home to Florida. The inherently Indonesian look of the furnishings is neither overwhelming nor overly ethnic, placed as they are within the context of the modernist building with its purity of form and open outlook. The solid shapes of the wooden dining table and benches are square and heavy, but they have been given plenty of room to breathe within the open air spaces of

left: A pair of benches made from salvaged wood form the seating for the dining area on the veranda. The table is reclaimed teak. The family live outside for much of the year, and eating outside in the summer dining room is cool and pleasant in the sultry Florida evenings.

the top-floor veranda, and the naturally dark tropical wood resonates comfortably with the banana and coconut palms that jostle for space just the other side of the railings.

Another of Max Strang's main design influences is the work of the Sri Lankan architect Geoffrey Bawa, whose designs evokes the pleasure of the senses so necessary to an appreciation of the climate and landscape of the tropics. Open, airy structures and an acute sensitivity to the environment characterize Bawa's buildings, and these guiding principles have been hugely influential in the construction of this striking Coconut Grove house.

right: More than in other places, the environment informs the architecture in the steamy heat of the tropics and a single heliconium flower decorates the dining table, bringing the exotic planting inside.

left: "Board and batten" white paneling used throughout the house balances the proportions of the rooms and adds texture to plain stretches of wall. Found in many original Coconut Grove houses, it's a style of wall covering that the Strangs found in the 1920s cottage in the garden and wanted to reproduce for its sense of timelessness.

right: The long, open-air terrace relies purely on the juxtaposition of textures for its beauty; rusty exposed structural steel girders, silvery-white ipe decking, Florida keystone copings, and white paneling build a layering of textures that is magical and daring.

rough with the smooth

Achieving authenticity of materials means using stone, wood, concrete, and glass in ways that are informed by their relevance to a building. The rawness and texture of a stone chimney breast is part of the fabric, but when left exposed speaks volumes about the local environment and the history of the culture. Oolite limestone is dug from the site whenever foundations are excavated in the Coconut Grove area, and has been a traditionally popular building material. Although white when it is first exposed to the air, the highly textured limestone takes on an ocher tinge within a few months. The stone was used inside and out at the Strang house partly for its texture and color, but also so that resources could be sourced locally to prevent too much carrying of materials. Set against the white paneled walls, the contrast of textures in the living room is striking.

below left: Light falls onto the rough surface of the limestone and the geometric planes of white-painted paneling alike, but the difference between the two throws the natural texture of the stone into strong relief.

right: The concrete floor that runs through the ground floor living spaces was put down by the contractors, but when polished and finished with a high gloss sealant it looks sophisticated and sleek.

below: Wherever you are in the house, you are never more than twelve feet from a window, all of which open onto the tropical gardens. Every frame has been darkened with an ebony stain, which underlines the simplicity of the white paneled walls.

white on wood

The ceilings in the master bedroom and its en-suite bathroom are unusually high, reaching nearly ten feet, and white-painted wooden paneling has been cleverly used here to lower the apparent height in these rooms, as elsewhere in the house. The eye-line travels effortlessly around at the same height in both rooms, following the divisions of the floor-to-ceiling windows, and strong horizontals are emphasized again in the stained wood paneling over the bed and bath. This is a useful design device that gives a wall more apparent width, and balances out the proportions of a very high room. Ebony-stained pine forms the bed head, and the deep color of the wood resonates with that of the window frames.

left: With such a dark surround, the understated textures of the white walls and bed linen look especially luminous.

right: The walnut stain of the bathroom paneling is quieter and warmer than the black wall above the bed, and the grain of the wood forms a subtle texture. The slightly battered vintage bathtub came from the garden cottage.

riverhouse

On the slopes above Hout Bay, near Cape Town, next to the Oranjekloof Nature Reserve, an extraordinary house nestles close to the Disa river with uninterrupted views of the forest and mountains. The house was conceived by Lisa May, a healer and counselor who, working with intuition rather than drawing skills, laid out bricks on the ground to indicate wall positions and room sizes. With a carefully-chosen team of local artisans and a building team from Germany, the house grew organically over nearly three years. Riverhouse seems to have grown naturally out of the ground. There are literally no straight lines, and the textures of the wood and stone and the undulating shapes of the building fit perfectly with the ethos of relaxation and meditation.

left: The pool area is curved to resemble a river bed, with stones brought from Hout Bay and a waterfall that tumbles out of the house wall. The sandstone used for cladding the walls is naturally textured and appears pale and white in the brilliant sunshine.

below right: The inside of the shower, like the rest of the house, is all curves and the whole area is finished by hand with a sica screed. The view from the shower, of the mountains and waterfall in the nature reserve, is spectacular.

below: Stepping out of the shower, it's only a few steps down to the blue water of the natural pool below. Inside and out blend without apparent boundaries through the wall of glass.

African thatch is an ideal way to keep a building cool in summer and warm in winter, and houses all over the Cape have roofs constructed in this way. Thick layers of natural reeds repel water and fend off the blazing heat of the African sun. It's an ancient art, and one that needs specialist designers to plan the complicated trusses needed to construct a curving roof line. May visualized a roof with more than usually undulating shapes when she created Riverhouse, in line with her concept for a home inspired in part by the creative and spiritual ideas of the architect Antonio Gaudi, the philosopher Rudolf Steiner, and the psychiatrist Carl Jung. The final, stunning design was the result of many hours of research and reflection. The supporting timbers for both roofs are made using sarinta, a much harder wood than the traditional poplar that is conventionally used, with the tree trunks left in all their natural beauty.

right: Many of the wardrobes in the bedrooms were made using bamboo grown on the land surrounding the house. The richly textured bamboo echoes the surface of the reed thatch of the roof.

below left: In the heat of summer, May decamps to the gazebo that has no walls, just a sturdy thatched roof supported on sarinta trunks. It's a cool place to work, where the river-cooled air wafts through the open sides. The pale planked floor of the gazebo reflects light upward onto the textured underside of the thatch.

below: The master bedroom has spectacular views across the untouched territory of the Oranjekloof Nature Reserve, and all the glass had to be specially shaped to fit the hand-carved window frames.

organically shaped

The original and unusual conception of the building is nowhere more in evidence than at the front of the house. The smooth adobe walls are punctuated by a facing of limestone and small windows, none of which are the same, and the house presents a unique, highly personal use of forms and materials. During the construction, May consulted a highly creative team of craftsmen and artisans, all of whom were selected for their expertise as well as their ability to work creatively when interpreting her ideas. She collaborated with designer John Barrett on the original concept, whose eco-friendly, sustainable buildings range from a whaler's cottage on the beach at Church Haven, to an entire village on the Big Five Game Reserve. The deep, curved entrance shades an inner area faced with limestone, and the gnarled trunk of an entire tree is exposed next to the contemporary glass entrance doors. Much of the complex woodwork was executed by carpenter Craig Bromwell, and the window frames, doors, and door frames are all hand-carved from a variety of natural woods which have been left in their natural state and oiled.

right: The smoothness of the adobe walls on the exterior is gradually acquiring a patina of varying shades and textures as it weathers and forms tiny cracks and fissures in the underlying layers.

The structure of Riverhouse is so unique and original that building it was, by necessity, a symbiotic process between the work teams and the designer. Communication was essential if the organic forms were to work in a practical way, so May selected artisans that would be able to take her ideas and work creatively within their own discipline. From the engineers and bricklayers, to the plasterers and plumbers, everyone was involved in the final outcome, and May describes the finished house as being "co-created." The impressive, double-height living space perfectly illustrates the result of this cooperation as the intrinsic quality of every tree, branch, and stone has been integrated in a natural relationship.

left: Each of the stair treads that lead from the ground floor is made from a thick chunk of stone pine, and the light fitting in the hallway, just seen beyond the staircase, has been constructed from a star shape of natural bamboo.

right: The close connection between the house and the landscape is evident in the textures and forms of every element. Running through the core of the house, the supporting post is formed from the trunk of a one-hundred-year-old poplar tree, found dying in the garden.

left: While Lisa May was involved with building Riverhouse, the family lived in the annexe, a purpose-built, five-bedroom cottage built on a budget with recycled and salvaged materials. The sunken bath has a standard shower, but in place of faucets or taps, a steel fountain allows water to flow freely.

right: The walls throughout the cottage have been colored with paints from the Earthcote range—textured paints that are designed to enhance surface. It is a finish that gives a matt, soft look to the walls. The mosaic bath, with its curving shape, has a coiled serpent molded into the side, symbolizing protection, fertility and Gaia, the goddess of the Earth.

shack chic

left: Sunlight filters through mesh screens pinned over roof lights in the roof and a bead curtain hangs at the long window over the double sinks. Both serve to soften the glare of the sun and allow a soft luminosity to gleam along the surfaces.

below: Portents of Riverhouse style are seen in the handmade cabinet frames, each one slightly different from its neighbor. The supporting post in the corner came from an old floating jetty in Cape Town harbor. Behind the cabinets, a light well has been built round a growing tree, forming a tiny courtyard.

Recycled bricks, slabs of slate, and corrugated iron sheets have all been pressed into service in the annexe kitchen, now used solely for guests. The natural materials give the kitchen an uncompromisingly utilitarian air, although the new gas hob and white ceramic sinks are features found in many modern kitchens. The charm comes from the way the bricks and the distressed window frames still have splashes of white paint left from a previous incarnation, and the rough-and-ready cabinets made from simple frames have corrugated sheets tacked behind the fronts. The wooden shelves, suspended from tension wires dropped from the ceiling, have solved the question of how to light the space. Chrome rails have been fixed underneath, with moveable spotlights fitted at intervals.

havana style

Kalk Bay is a fashionable fishing village that stretches along the coast just south of Cape Town, and is crowded with antique and craft shops, coffee bars and restaurants. "Cape to Cuba" must be one of the most original and exciting places to stop by for coffee or lunch, or to visit in the evening for Cuban music and authentic food. A former railway goods shed now converted into a restaurant/bar, the ambience inside and out is achieved with vintage Cuban furniture and an eclectic and relaxed approach.

left: In the yard outside, the white sand is soft underfoot, and a battered table is shaded with dried palm fronds tied loosely together to form a natural parasol. The white textures of the old furniture and planters are set against a fence roughly painted with the Cuban flag.

right: A weathered park seat was once painted sky blue, but the years have stripped it of all but the most worn out remnants of color. The rusty table is similarly distressed, but the setting takes its mood from the faded grandeur of old Havana and has a similar glamour and style.

above: To light this romantic aluminum gazebo, a decorative Moroccan lantern holds a candle aand gives the pavilion a warm glow at night.

left: Built into the side of a steep hillside, the designer of this Cape Town garden has made extra space by building a gazebo on a tall wooden platform and linked it to the main garden via a rope bridge. The white of the bridge is reflected in the sheen of the metal which catches the light as it filters through the trees.

summer living

One of the joys of summer must be spending as much time as possible out of doors, and connecting with nature in all its aspects is only possible when the house is abandoned in favor of a shady spot under the trees or a well-placed seat from which to enjoy the warmth of the first rays of the sun. A cleverly designed garden will dramatically increase the pleasure of living outside by providing different areas for a variety of activities. A cobbled or paved patio in the shade makes the ideal place to site a table for eating outside and a sun-drenched lawn or timber deck provides just the spot for placing a pair of sun loungers or deckchairs.

When it comes to designing a new garden or refiguring an existing plot, the use of garden structures like gazebos, pergolas, or trellis will artificially create shade if vines, clematis, or similar climbing plants are allowed to clamber up and cover the framework. A wooden pergola or trellis can easily be made at home, but a more decorative metal gazebo is usually bought readymade and assembled on site. The use of garden features will help lift the eye skyward by introducing verticals into the planting, especially useful if the garden is attached to a tall house. A helpful way to increase the sense of space in a small garden is to place a small pavilion at the end of a walkway or path where the eye can come to rest.

above right: Long exposed to the sun and rain of the Cape, an old pine table has developed deep fissures in its wood, bleached almost white by the sun and forming a beautifully textured surface.

right: Decorative white cobbles have been laid in the courtyard and Mediterranean plants shade an outdoor dining room, making it an ideal spot for lingering over lunch.

acknowledgments

I would like to thank all the people who helped me work on this exciting project, and to all those who helped me find locations in Fort Walton Beach, Miami, Santorini, and Cape Town.

To Carey McWhorter, Abby Kellett, Tara Sloggett, George Alexandrou at Luxury Retreats, and Lisa Martin at Amazing Spaces. Without your help I would have found it difficult, if not impossible, to find such a wide variety of fabulous and unique houses.

To those who were generous enough to let us into your homes to take the photographs—Terri de Sanary, Candace and Jamey Price, Ken Ganeaux and Keith Flippo, Andrew King and Carey Hero King, and Royce Kershaw, Jeff Morr, Terence Riley and John Bennett, and Max and Tamara Strang.

To Ester Clark, and Brigitte for meeting us and opening up Villa Io and Blue Angel Villa, and to Charlotte, Dave, and Ingemar for making us so welcome at Sunset Beach Guest House.

To my editor Gillian Haslam for her guidance, to Christine Wood for her wonderful design, and to picture editor Sally Powell. And, as always, many thanks to my publisher, Cindy Richards, for her support on this and other projects.

To Mark Scott, who did such brilliant work in taking the wonderful photographs that have made the book so rich and inspiring.